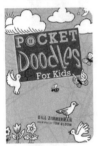

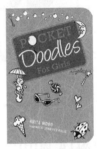

Collect Them All!

COWBOY doodles

ANITA WOOD
DRAWINGS BY **KEV BROCKSCHMIDT**

GIBBS SMITH
TO ENRICH AND INSPIRE HUMANKIND

Manufactured in Altona, Manitoba, Canada
in May 2013 by Friesens

First Edition
17 16 15 14 13   5 4 3 2 1

Text © 2013 Anita Wood
Illustrations © 2013 Kev Brockschmidt

Published by
Gibbs Smith
P.O. Box 667
Layton, Utah 84041

1.800.835.4993 orders
www.gibbs-smith.com

Designed by Renee Bond
Gibbs Smith books are printed on either recycled, 100% post-
consumer waste, FSC-certified papers or on paper produced
from sustainable PEFC-certified forest/controlled wood
source. Learn more at www.pefc.org.

ISBN 13: 978-1-4236-3392-1

For Pappy and Snoose.

All cowboy and all heart.

There's a new sheriff in town.
Finish your shiny badge.

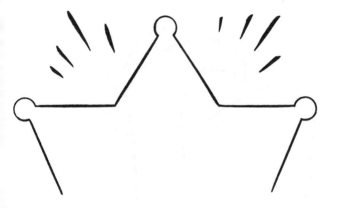

Don't clean your work boots; you'll take the luck off! Give these boots a good layer of mud and dirt.

Give each of these buckaroos a different mustache.

Ouch! You just sat down on a
cactus. Draw the spiky little devil.

Phew! You just missed steppin' into
a fresh cow pie. Draw it here.

Design a pair of chinks (shorter chaps).

Give this hardworkin'
cowboy some hat hair.

A cowboy's best friend is his trusty steed. Draw and name your ridin' buddy.

Turn this horseshoe into a
very bowlegged cowboy.

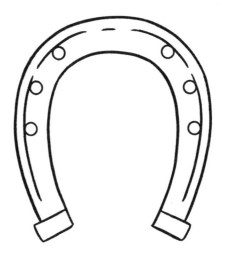

Add some fancy tooling (leatherwork designs) to this saddle.

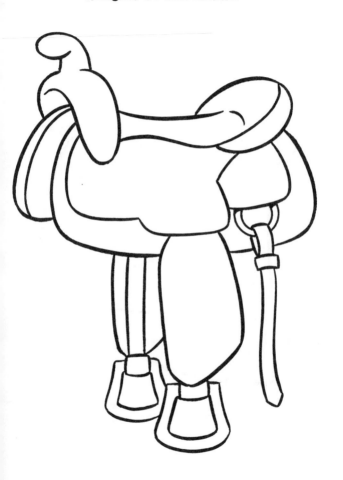

Doodle a design on this saddle blanket.

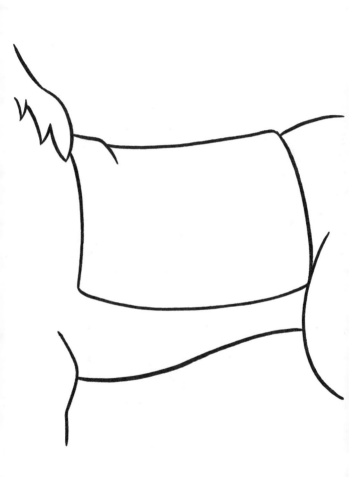

Give this singing cowboy a guitar so he can sing the dogies (calves) to sleep.

"Oh, give me a home where the buffalo roam . . ." What else is roaming there?

"Hey, barkeep. Pour me a tall, cool glass of sarsaparilla." Fill the mug with this foamy root beer-flavored drink.

This poor cowboy's been ridin' drag (behind the group) in the roundup. Give him a face full of grit and dirt.

Draw the rider that's trying to break this bucking bronco.

My heroes have always been
cowboys. Who are some of yours?

You've got the biggest spread around. Doodle the name of your ranch over the entrance.

Design a branding iron for your ranch.

Gotta go! Build yerself a fancy
one-seat or two-seat outhouse.

Something purty is growing out
of this dried-up horse puckey.

This belt buckle is bigger 'n you! Doodle a design on it.

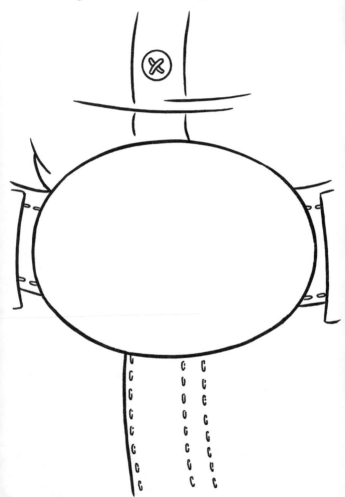

Draw a picture of your trusty cowdog.

Buffalo chips don't belong at a picnic! Pack this basket with some tastier vittles (food).

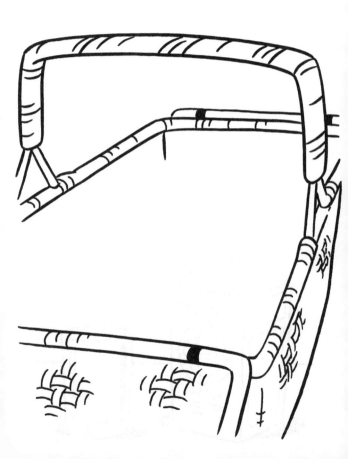

Got cow juice? Draw yourself
with a milk mustache.

This cowboy's horse just stopped
suddenly. What did he get tossed into?

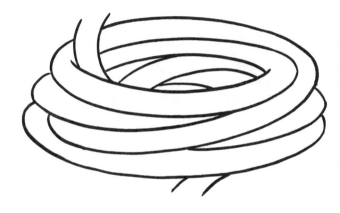

This coil of rope is really a snake getting
ready to strike! Give it a head and a tail.

Doodle a funny epitaph (saying)
on this tombstone.

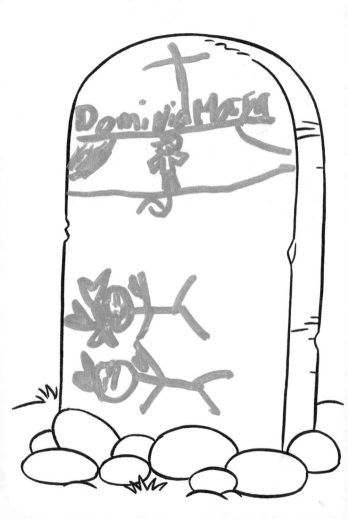

Add some more creepy-looking tombstones in this bone orchard.

The bandito you were chasing lost his sombrero. Draw it here along with the bullet hole you just shot into it!

$$ Reward! Draw yourself on this wanted poster along with your outlaw name.

Shootin' iron. Custom design your
trusty rifle and scabbard.

You've taken up knapping (shaping)
your own flint arrowheads.
Draw your points here.

Make a brand that symbolizes
broken hearts.

Gone a-courtin'. Draw a picture of your best gal or beau.

Gone huntin' and bagged a huge elk.
Draw the prize-winning antlers.

It's dawn and the rooster's crowing
"time to git up." Draw this noisy old bird.

Cowgirls often wear different colored socks
on each foot for good luck at the rodeo.
Give this little gal some lucky socks.

Fancy kickers. Give these boots a one-of-a-kind design.

Who will help this damsel in distress?

Every cowboy movie hero has
a sidekick. Who's yours?

Add a steer skull and horns to this bale of hay so you can practice your ropin' skills.

RODEO CHAMP

You just won the county rodeo
championship. Draw your prize.

Eating a hot dog before competing at the rodeo is said to bring good luck! Pile on your favorite toppings.

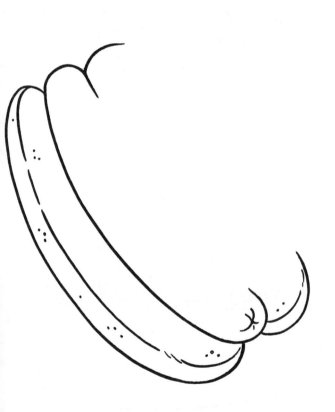

This rodeo clown, or barrel man,
needs his face painted.

There's a secret compartment
in your saddle horn. What
have you stashed there?

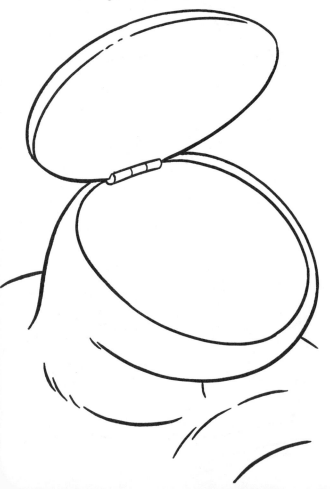

Gold fever! Draw the entrance to your secret gold mine.

This old miner has been in the desert way too long! Draw the mirage that he's crawling to get to.

All tied up. Decorate the slide on this bolo tie and add some shiny tips.

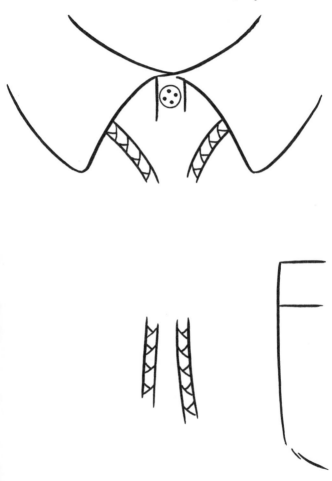

Doodle a design on this hatband.

Draw the big old woolly sheep this little mutton buster is trying to hang on to.

Give this little filly a makeover by
adding braids and bows to her mane.

Make up a scary ghost story to
tell around the campfire.

Wild Bill Hickok, Old West gunfighter, scout, and lawman, was shot and killed while playing poker. It is said that he was holding an ace of spades, ace of clubs, eight of spades, and eight of clubs, commonly known as the dead man's hand. What do you think the fifth card was?

Draw! A shiny pair of six-shooters.

Custom design a holster for
them fancy shooters.

Who's yippin' at the full moon?

A cowboy's alarm clock is the sun just starting to sneak up over the eastern sky. Draw Mr. Sun as he breaks the day.

Give this barbed wire a new twist by adding your own kind of spikes and prickly things.

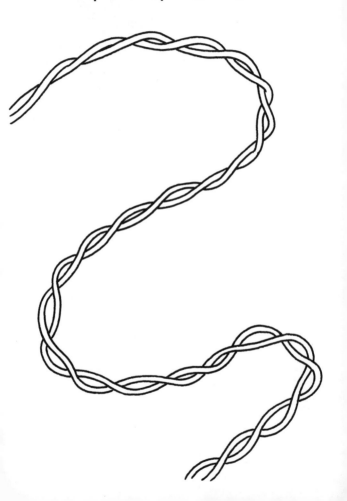

What has this cowgirl caught in her lasso?

Decorate this pair of moccasins with some fringe and a beaded design.

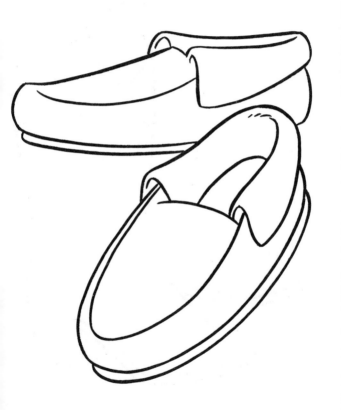

Boot candy. Glam up these boots with some cowgirl bling.

Now that's a horse of a different color! Doodle some unusual markings on this little mare and make her your favorite color.

What is this curious little
billy goat munching on?

Tossed into the pokey and you don't know for how long; might as well be comfortable. Decorate your jail cell.

Design a dugout (canoe) for a swift getaway down the river.

"Howdy." Who just passed
you on the trail?

Gone to his reward, old Slim got his wish and was buried with his boots on, but they didn't put him in very deep. Draw his boots.

This rodeo champion has "earned his spurs!" Doodle a fancy design on this pair.

Give these spur straps a
design to match.

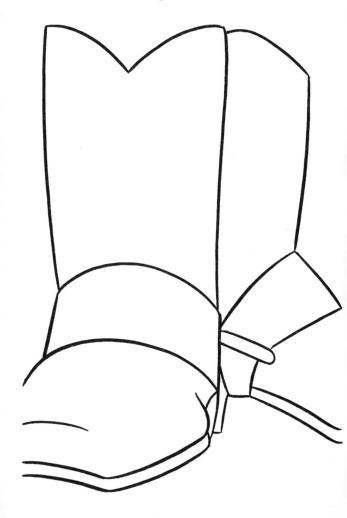

Throw another log on this fire before it burns out.

Make a cattle brand out of this word and letters.

There's a storm a-brewin'. Fill
the sky with dark thunderclouds
and lightning bolts.

Hang a horseshoe over the door for luck.
Make sure the two ends are pointing up
so none of the good luck will run out.

What does Cookie have simmering in the pot for supper?

This good old boy just had a cup of "cowboy coffee." You can tell because his teeth are full of coffee grounds! Draw his grimy grin.

Masked bandits are giving chase
to this stagecoach. Draw them.

Have you ever seen a necktie in the shape of a cactus? Add one to this shirt.

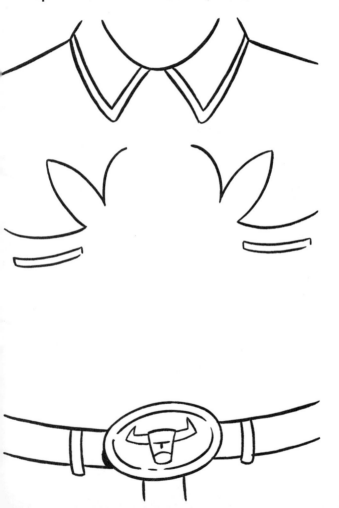

Give this belt buckle some sparkly jewels
and a design fit for a rodeo princess.

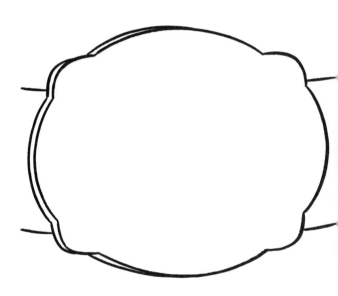

Change this "C" into a brand by adding
lines, circles, or your initials to it.

Miss Daisy is missing her cowbell.

Sweet treats at the county fair.
Top this paper cone with a
huge puff of cotton candy.

With a yip and a holler, who's testing their skill on the mechanical bull?

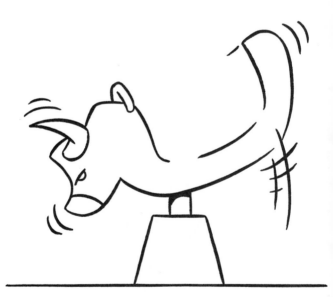

These woolly chaps are missing their fur!

Dress this "city slicker" up in some cowboy duds.

Soo-ee! Draw the cute little porker that's about to win the pig racing contest.

Cowboy ABCs

A is for Armadillo. Finish adding the rest of this little fellow's armor.

B is for Breakfast Biscuits, Beans, and Bacon. Fill up this hungry cowpoke's plate.

C is for Cowboy Code. Finish adding your own list of "Cowboy Commandments."

COWBOY COMMANDMENTS

★ A cowboy must always tell the truth.
★ A cowboy must be a good worker.

D is for Desert. Add some cactus, dried bones, snakes, and other things you might find in the desert.

E is for Eight seconds. This rider is trying to stay on for eight seconds before getting tossed off. Draw the big old bull he's ridin'.

F is for Fiddle. Give this old-timer a fiddle so everyone can kick up their heels.

G is for Giddyap. Draw your
very first stick horse.

H is for Hat. Doodle each of these Western characters a different hat. Cattle Baron, Sheriff, Rancher,

Gambler, Texas Ranger, Vaquero.

I is for American Indian. Give this chief a big feathered headdress.

J is for Jingle bob, a piece of metal that dangles next to the spur wheel that makes a ringing sound when moved. Add a jingle bob to this spur.

K is for Klondike Gold Rush. Fill this pan with some big gold nuggets.

L is for Long johns. This pair of underwear is missing its flap!

M is for Mesa. Draw some smoke
signals coming from yonder mesa.

N is for Nighthawk. This cowboy has to stay up all night watching the herd. How will you help him stay awake?

O is for Outfit. Finish drawing the rest of this cowboy's pickup truck (outfit).

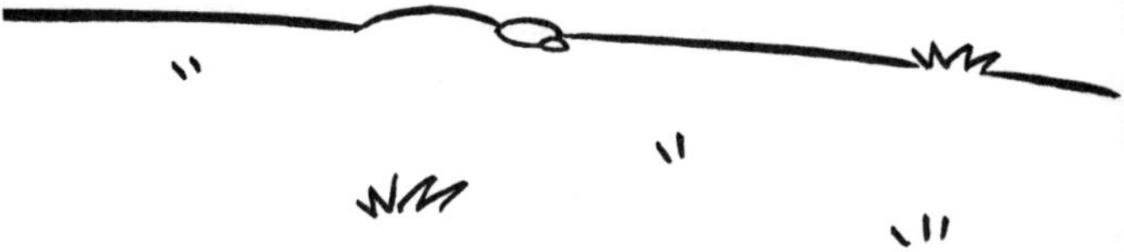

P is for Prairie dog. Draw the little feller peeping out of his hole in the ground.

Q is for Queen of the rodeo.
Give her a sparkly crown.

R is for Raging River. How are you going to get across, by bridge or ferry?

S is for Spurs that jingle jangle.
How many points will you put
on the rowel (wheel)?

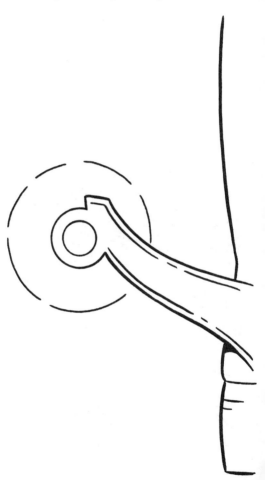

T is for Tractor. What is this tractor pulling behind it?

U is for sleeping Under the moon and stars. Fill the night sky with these shiny beacons.

V is for Varmint. Draw the ratty critter that has helped itself to your food supply.

W is for Weather vane. Add one to the top of this barn.

X is for eXtra cold nights. Draw the icicles hanging from these elk antlers.

Y is for Yee-haw. What is this junior rodeo rider hanging onto for dear life?

Z is for well-deserved ZZZs at the end of a long day. Give this tired cowpoke a nice bunk to rest in.

Help get these cattle to the stockyards.

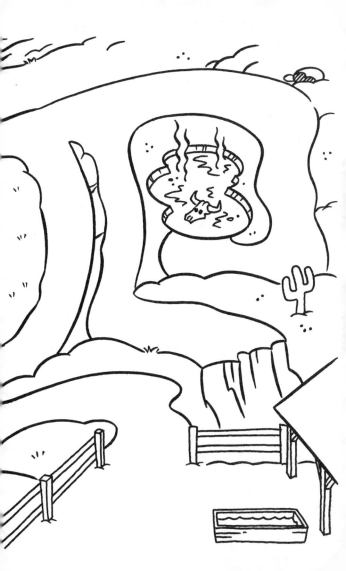

Add the different colored spots and splotches to this pinto pony.

What has spooked this horse?

Add some conchos (decorative silver buttons) to these chaps.

Turn this spur rowel into
a blingy necklace.

Decorate the flags these flag riders
at the rodeo are presenting.

What is chasing this rodeo clown around the arena?

First love. Draw this little
buckarette's pony.

This poor old fool's gone loopy for the farmer's daughter. Draw the lovely lass.

Add your own rules to this list.

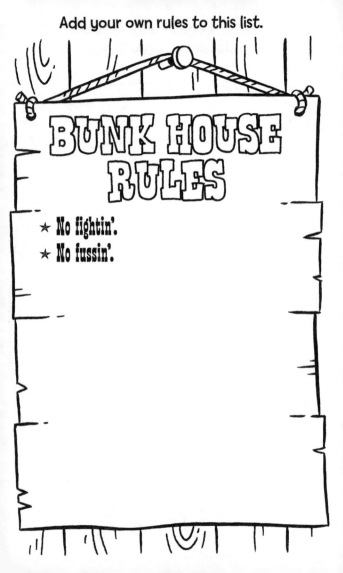

BUNK HOUSE RULES

★ No fightin'.
★ No fussin'.

Who is one of your favorite movie-time cowboys?

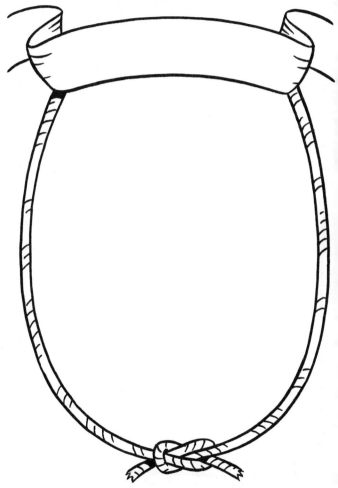

This desperado is "wanted" on
both sides of the border.

Time to hit the trail and make tracks.
Let's saddle up your trusty horse.

Build a desert snowman using tumbleweeds.

Draw the ghosts that have taken up residence in this abandoned town.

What kind of tracks are you following?

Who or what has little "sure-shot" got lined up in her sights?

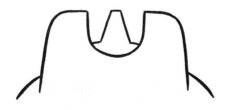

Snap happy! Give this pearl-
button shirt a fancy design.

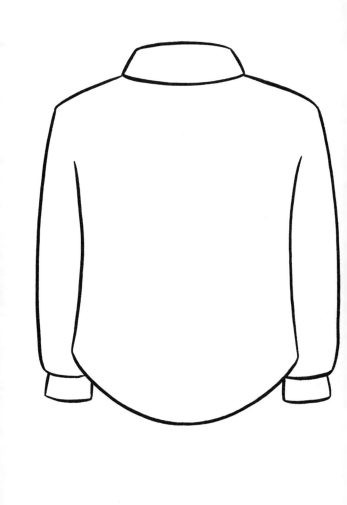

This cowgirl is running a barrel race.
Draw the barrel she's turning 'round.

This little cowboy needs some help mounting his horse. Draw a bucket for him to stand on.

This little cowgirl is competing in the goat tail-tying contest. Draw the goat she's tying a ribbon on.

Who is crossing the finish line in first place at the stick pony race?

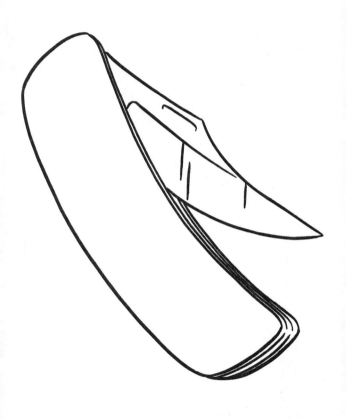

Doodle a design on this pocketknife.

Give this buckle and belt
tip matching designs.

Draw the flash flood rattling its way through this gulch.

Everything's bigger in Texas. Doodle some big old freckles and buckteeth on this feller.

Cowboy of legend and folklore Pecos Bill is said to have once lassoed a tornado and ridden it from Kansas clear to California. Draw old Bill riding the tornado.

Pecos Bill's sweetheart was Slue-Foot Sue, who rode a giant catfish down the Rio Grande. Draw Sue on her fish.

Pecos Bill's legendary horse was named Widow-Maker. When Slue-Foot Sue tried to ride him on her wedding day to Bill, Widow-Maker tossed her so high she almost hit the moon! Draw Sue.

The legend of Pecos Bill grew out of the imaginations of the ranch hands who tried to outdo each other by telling tall tales. Can you write a tall tale of your own?

Help this cowboy find the stray calf.

Do you have a lucky pair of jeans?
Draw them here, holes and all!

Give this cowgirl some wrist candy.

This old boy got stuck with shoveling duties. What's he shoveling out and cleaning up?

Finish drawing the chuck wagon.

Every trail has some puddles and this one is full of 'em! Draw a bunch.

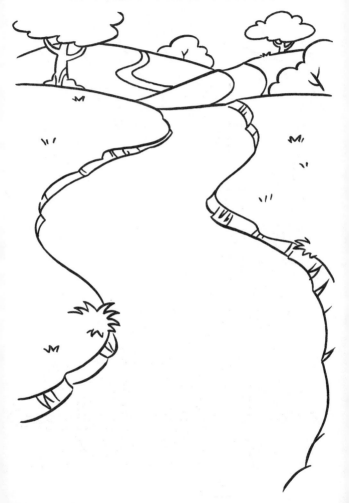

It's pouring down and rainin' sheets.
Give this cowpuncher a rain slicker.

Draw the calf that just got caught
during the tie-down roping contest.

This little gal has just earned the title
All-Around Cowgirl at the state rodeo
finals. Draw the fancy saddle she won.

What has this buffalo herd on the run?

Setting up for the flag race. Draw one of the big barrels; add a bucket on top and stick a flag in it.

It's time for the steer undecorating
event, and this cowgirl has to untie the
ribbon around this fast-moving critter!
Draw the steer she's chasing and
the ribbon tied around him.

"A cowboy hat looks silly on anybody who ain't a cowboy." Who's wearing this hat?

Use it up, wear it out, make it do,
or do without. Put some patches
over the holes in these jeans.

Sittin' tall in the saddle, this cowboy is riding off into the sunset. Draw the sun as it starts to set.

Give this long, tall Texan a
big white horse to ride.

Draw the purty little thing this cowboy's spinning around on the dance floor.

Doodle all the hearts this
little cowgirl has stolen.

Your prize bull just won Grand Champion
at the county fair. Draw the big ol' ribbon
and rosette that comes with this title.

"There ain't a hoss that can't be rode.
There ain't a rider that can't be throwed."
Who just flew out of chute #3?

"It don't take a genius to spot a goat in a flock of sheep." Give this lonely sheep some friends and don't forget the goat!

Give this old Texas cowboy a buckskin shirt and leggings, complete with fringe.

It's wash day on the ranch. What's hangin' on the clothesline?

"One, two, draw!" the good guy sheriff and notorious bad guy outlaw who've met in the middle of town for a showdown.

Who is your favorite legendary outlaw?

How much money did the bank
robbers get away with? Fill the
bags with bills and coins.

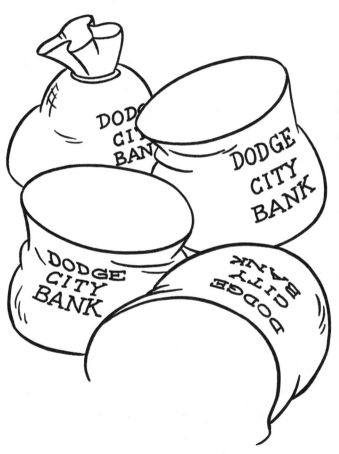

Yippie-yi-o! Draw the "ghost riders" on their fire-snorting horses.

It's feeding time for this little calf.
Since momma ain't around, let's hook
this youngster up with a bottle.

Draw the little kitty who's
keeping the cowboy company
while on line camp duty.

Add some grass and wildflowers to this Montana meadow.

Bath time! Who just plunged into this chilly creek?

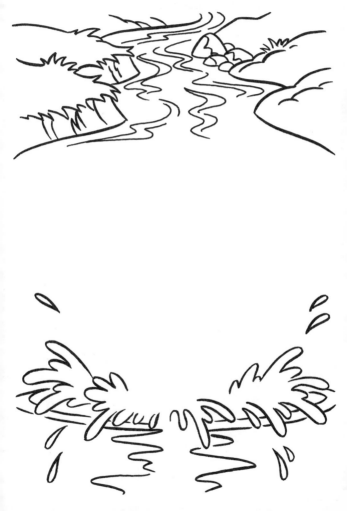

Draw the famous Teton Mountain Range that serves as a majestic backdrop to the wild Snake River.

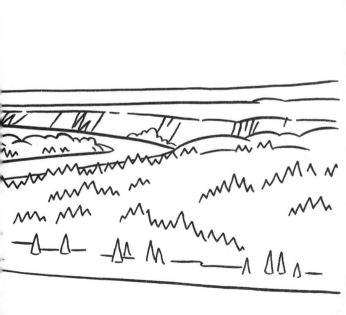

Draw the pesky no-see-ums snacking
away on this buckaroo's ear.

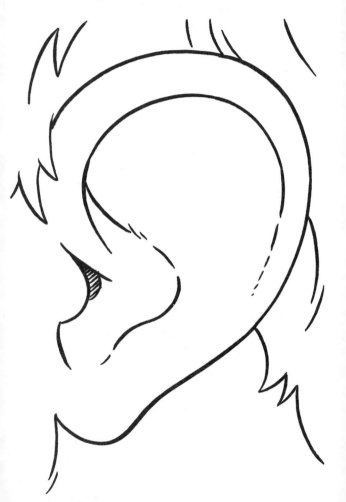

This old vaquero's face has been tanned deep by many years in the sun. Give him a bunch of wrinkles.

Help load this old pickup
truck with hay bales.

Add the wheels to this buckboard
(wagon) and fill it with supplies
like bags of sugar and flour.

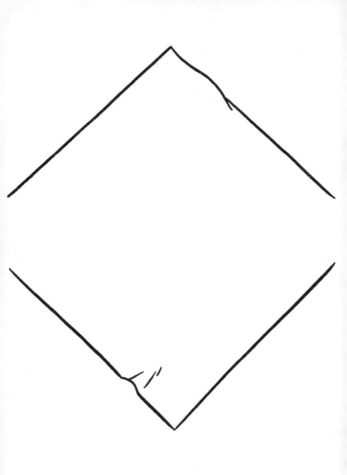

Decorate this bandana with
some Western symbols such
as boots, hats, and spurs.

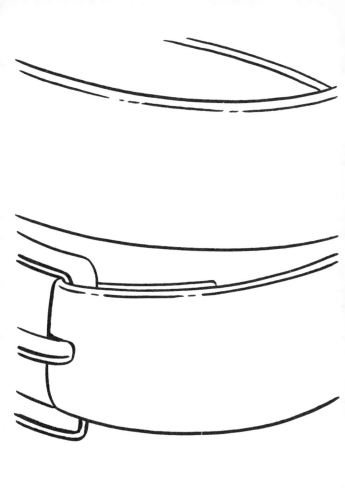

Doodle your name and a design
on this leather belt.

Help finish building the bunkhouse.

Add the vane and sails to this windmill.

Give this deep-sea riding cowboy a seahorse.

Draw the steer this bulldogger is trying to wrestle to the ground.

"Hoo" is wearing these boots?

What has this old turkey vulture got its eye on for supper?

It's huntin' season. Set up
your campsite and tent.

Make a branding iron that symbolizes twin pine trees.

Also known as the "iron horse," draw the steam engine that's puffing and chugging along these railroad tracks.

Aww ... cute little bear cub.
You can bet mama ain't too far
behind. Draw mama bear.

Fill the sky with wild geese on their fall migration.

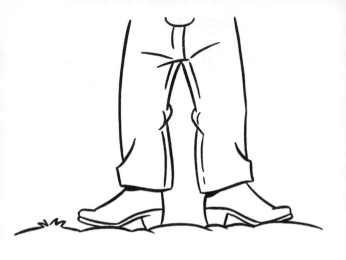

Give this cowboy drifter
some roots under his boots
to help settle him down.

Nature is often a lonesome cowboy's companion as he drifts from place to place. Draw some of his wild friends.

What is hitchin' a ride on the back of this old bull?

Add a yoke (wooden collar) to this team of oxen.

Draw the wanted poster for "Bandit Queen," Belle Starr.

"Reach for the sky!" Who got
the draw on this rustler?

Cowboy Word Search

q	d	r	i	v	e	o	e	d	o	r	s
d	b	l	p	r	i	s	w	l	q	c	p
n	n	r	o	h	g	n	o	l	l	m	a
k	d	o	a	b	o	f	e	o	a	u	h
p	r	p	c	n	d	l	d	r	u	h	c
u	o	i	v	m	d	f	e	d	j	g	d
d	v	n	f	d	t	q	w	e	u	e	f
n	e	g	a	c	n	o	r	b	s	s	q
u	r	s	c	a	t	t	l	e	v	p	t
o	u	t	f	i	t	d	r	g	n	u	u
r	h	c	n	a	r	t	r	s	c	r	l
a	r	a	r	a	n	g	e	e	h	s	n

brand	roping	dogie	saddle
drive	chaps	bronc	mare
desert	outfit	dust	drover
cattle	bedroll	roundup	longhorn
rodeo	ranch	spurs	range

100

This little cowpoke has some money burning a hole in his pocket and he's looking to buy some candy.
Fill the jars with your favorite kinds.

What kind of pies are cooling on the windowsill?

Finish drawing the thief who is
stealing one of those pies.

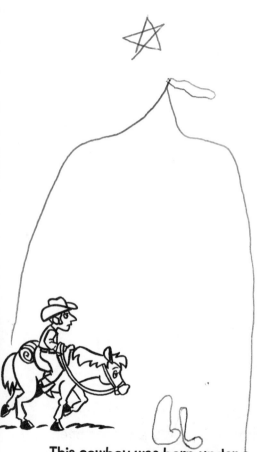

This cowboy was born under a
wanderin' star. Where has it led him?

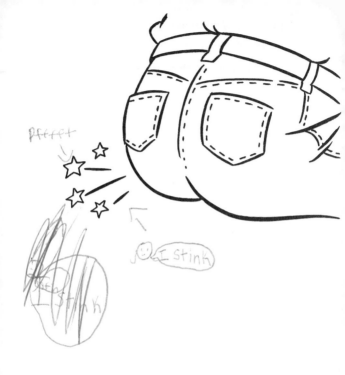

This tired old cowpuncher has been way too long in the saddle. Give him a cushy pillow to rest his saddle-sore bottom on.

Draw an old Western town at its busiest time. Why is everyone crowding the streets?

There's a red-tailed hawk perched on the fence post. Draw Mr. Hawk and the unlucky mouse he's got his eye on.

Help finish mending the fence.

You're invited to a shotgun wedding!
Draw the reluctant groom and his bride.

Draw the queen of this buckaroo ball.

"Music hath charms to soothe the savage beast." Who or what has fallen under the spell of this piano player?

Draw the pile of bronc busters
this outlaw roan has piled up
in the corner of the corral.

This lucky cowboy ducked a punch.
What is this fist going to hit instead?

It's a necktie party (Hangman)! Find a friend or family member and decide which of you will think of a word and which of you will guess the letters. Try not to hang the poor fellow!

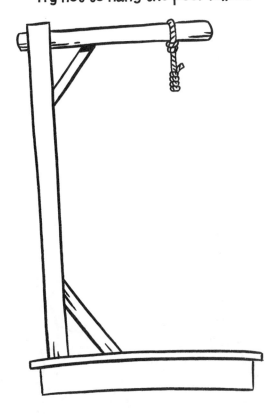

Make a cattle brand that shows a rocking star.

Doodle some antlers on this mounted moose head.

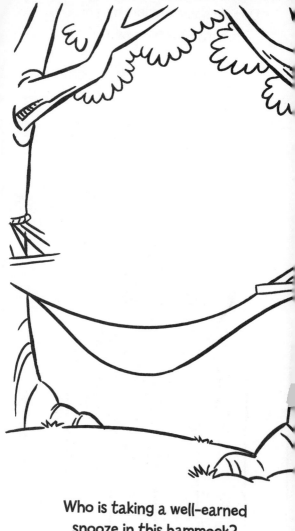

Who is taking a well-earned
snooze in this hammock?